READY, SET, GAME!

COMPUTER
GAMING

BY BETSY RATHBURN

BELLWETHER MEDIA • MINNEAPOLIS, MN

™

TORQUE brims with excitement
perfect for thrill-seekers of all kinds.
Discover daring survival skills, explore
uncharted worlds, and marvel at mighty
engines and extreme sports. In *Torque* books,
anything can happen. Are you ready?

This edition first published in 2021 by Bellwether Media, Inc.

No part of this publication may be reproduced in whole or in part without
written permission of the publisher. For information regarding permission,
write to Bellwether Media, Inc., Attention: Permissions Department,
6012 Blue Circle Drive, Minnetonka, MN 55343.

Library of Congress Cataloging-in-Publication Data

Names: Rathburn, Betsy, author.
Title: Computer gaming / by Betsy Rathburn.
Description: Minneapolis, MN : Bellwether Media, [2021] | Series:
    Torque: ready, set, game! | Includes bibliographical references and
    index. | Audience: Ages 7-12 | Audience: Grades 4-6 | Summary:
    "Amazing photography accompanies engaging information about
    computer gaming. The combination of high-interest subject matter and
    light text is intended for students in grades 3 through 7"– Provided
    by publisher.
Identifiers: LCCN 2020048051 (print) | LCCN 2020048052 (ebook)
    | ISBN 9781644874554 (library binding) | ISBN 9781648342486
    (paperback) | ISBN 9781648341328 (ebook)
Subjects: LCSH: Computer games–Juvenile literature. | Gaming
    industry–Juvenile literature.
Classification: LCC GV1469.27 .R38 2021 (print) | LCC GV1469.27
    (ebook) | DDC 794.8–dc23
LC record available at https://lccn.loc.gov/2020048051
LC ebook record available at https://lccn.loc.gov/2020048052

Editor: Elizabeth Neuenfeldt   Designer: Brittany McIntosh

Printed in the United States of America, North Mankato, MN.

TABLE OF CONTENTS

BLOCK
BY BLOCK

Enderman

Night is falling fast. You see an Enderman in the distance. Then, more monsters come into view. Creepers! Your weapons are not strong enough to fight them.

Instead, you take out your pickaxe.
You dig into a nearby mountain to build
a cave. You are safe until the monsters leave.
The world of *Minecraft* is full of danger!

COMPUTER GAMING HISTORY

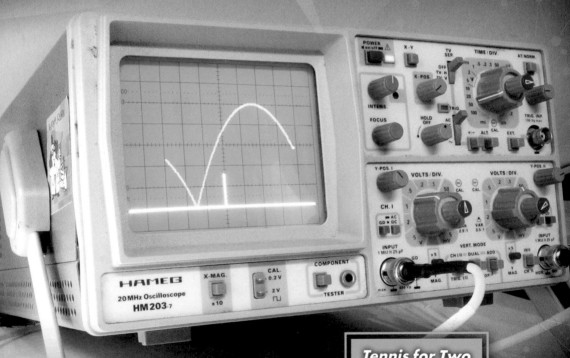

Tennis for Two model

People began making computer games in the mid-1900s. They were mostly used to show off

In 1958, *Tennis for Two* was among the first games made for the public. Players pressed buttons to bounce a ball across a screen! Many people lined up to play. But it was only available on one machine.

BERTIE THE BRAIN

Many early games were designed after existing games. In 1950, *Bertie the Brain* was the first tic-tac-toe computer game!

Bertie the Brain

COMPUTER GAMING TIMELINE

1958
Tennis for Two is one of the first computer games made for the public

1962
Spacewar! is the first game to be played on multiple computers

1970s
Personal computers allow people to play games at home

1971

Microprocessors lead to smaller and more affordable computers

1980

Mystery House is among the first computer games with graphics

1985
CD-ROMs are released, leading to more complex games

1993

Myst is released, becoming the best-selling computer game of the 1990s

In 1962, Steve Russell created *Spacewar!* It was the first computer game to be played on multiple computers. Still, it was mostly played by researchers. People could not get the game in their homes.

In 1971, **microprocessors** were introduced. These made computers smaller and more affordable. This led to more computer use and gaming throughout the 1970s and 1980s.

Spacewar!

Many early computer games were
text-based. Players answered questions and
typed commands to move through a story.
In 1980, *Mystery House* was among the first
games to include **graphics**!

TETRIS 99

Tetris was first created
for computers in 1984.
It has been ported to many
devices since then. Today,
Nintendo Switch users enjoy
playing *Tetris 99*!

Tetris 99

Donkey Kong

floppy disk

Later, popular **arcade** games were **ported** to computers. People inserted **floppy disks** to play games such as *Pac-Man* and *Donkey Kong*.

In 1985, **CD-ROMs** were released. They could store much more information than floppy disks. This led to more **complex** games!

The 1990s saw many popular games. *Civilization* and *StarCraft* were popular **strategy games**. People also enjoyed playing **simulation games** such as *RollerCoaster Tycoon*. The 1993 puzzle game *Myst* was very popular. It was the top-selling computer game in the 1990s!

CD-ROM

StarCraft

COMPUTER GRAPHICS THROUGH TIME

1958

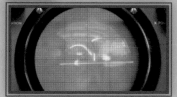

Tennis for Two

1971

Oregon Trail

1980

Mystery House

1984

Tetris

1989

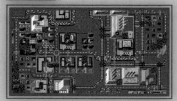

SimCity

1991

Civilization

1999

RollerCoaster Tycoon

2011

Minecraft

13

COMPUTER GAMING
TODAY

Minecraft

Computer games are still popular today.
Many are played online. Players connect on the
internet. The 2011 **sandbox game** *Minecraft*
lets people play together through online **servers**.

MMORPGs are popular online computer games, too. *World of Warcraft* is one of the most well-known MMORPGs. Millions of players have logged in since it started in 2004!

World of Warcraft

GAME SPOTLIGHT

GAME *Terraria*

YEAR 2011

TYPE sandbox

DESCRIPTION Players collect resources to craft weapons and other useful items as they explore the world.

Stardew Valley

People also play computer games offline.
In 2016, *Stardew Valley* was released. Players
build a farm and become friends with characters
in the game. It has been downloaded millions
of times!

In 2019, *Planet Zoo* was a big hit. Players collect animals to build zoos. *Tangle Tower* was also popular. Players find clues to solve a mystery!

POPULAR COMPUTER GAMES
(BY NUMBER OF GAMES SOLD)

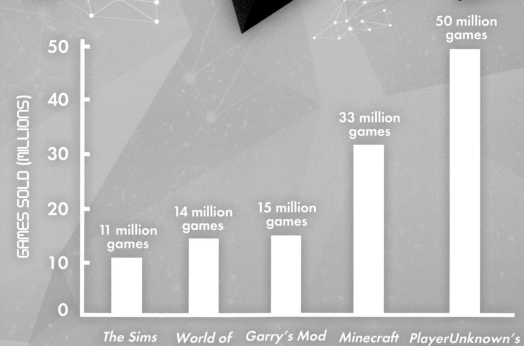

50 million games

33 million games

15 million games

14 million games

11 million games

GAMES SOLD (MILLIONS)

50

40

30

20

10

0

The Sims

World of Warcraft

Garry's Mod

Minecraft

PlayerUnknown's Battlegrounds

GAMES

THE COMPUTER GAMING COMMUNITY

Minecon

There are many events in the computer gaming community. *World of Warcraft* has an event each year. In 2020, players played head-to-head for $500,000 in prizes!

Gaming **conferences** are also common. In 2011, the first official Minecon was held. Fans dressed as their favorite *Minecraft* characters, met other players, and learned more about the game. The event is now held every year!

COMPUTER GAMING EVENT SPOTLIGHT

EVENT *Minecraft* Live (formerly Minecon)

HOST Mojang Studios

GAME *Minecraft*

YEAR FIRST HELD 2011

WHEN IT HAPPENS once per year

WHERE IT HAPPENS around the world and online

LEGO MINECRAFT

LEGO has released many *Minecraft* playsets. These let players build monsters, animals, and even a pirate ship!

There are many other ways to enjoy computer games. Game makers release special products. Fans can buy board games or collect models of their favorite characters.

Many of the world's most popular games are made for computers. People will enjoy computer games for years to come!

GLOSSARY

arcade—related to places where people can go to play games

CD-ROMs—discs that are read by lasers that store information for computers

complex—having many parts that work together

conferences—events in which people gather to learn about a certain subject

floppy disks—thin, plastic squares that store information for computers

graphics—images displayed on a computer screen

microprocessors—small chips that hold a computer's memory

MMORPGs—massively multiplayer online role-playing games; MMORPGs let players create and move around an online world with a character and interact with other players.

ported—adapted to be used on another gaming system

sandbox game—a game that does not have a set story; a sandbox game often includes tools that allow the player to change the game world.

servers—the main computers in networks that allow other computers to share information with one another

simulation games—games made to recreate something

strategy games—games that require careful planning to achieve goals

TO LEARN MORE

AT THE LIBRARY

Green, Sara. *Minecraft*. Minneapolis, Minn.: Bellwether Media, 2017.

Hansen, Dustin. *Game On!: Video Game History from Pong and Pac-Man to Mario, Minecraft, and More*. New York, N.Y.: Feiwel & Friends, 2016.

Rathburn, Betsy. *Online Gaming*. Minneapolis, Minn: Bellwether Media, 2021.

ON THE WEB

FACTSURFER

Factsurfer.com gives you a safe, fun way to find more information.

1. Go to www.factsurfer.com.

2. Enter "computer gaming" into the search box and click 🔍.

3. Select your book cover to see a list of related content.

INDEX